AF134543

Hamad Bin Khalifa University Press
P O Box 5825
Doha, Qatar

www.hbkupress.com

First published in Arabic by Hamad Bin Khalifa University Press, 2021.
Translation Copyright © Hamad Bin Khalifa University Press.

All rights reserved.

No part of this publication may be reproduced or transmitted in any form or by any means, electronic or mechanical, including photocopying, recording, or any information storage or retrieval system, without prior permission in writing from the publishers.

No responsibility for loss caused to any individual or organization acting on or refraining from action as a result of the material in this publication can be accepted by HBKU Press or the author.

First English edition, 2022

Hamad Bin Khalifa University Press

ISBN: 9789927155994

Printed in Doha-Qatar.

Qatar National Library Cataloging-in-Publication (CIP)

Ibrahim, Andalous, author.

[ماذا لو اختفت المدرسة!]. English

What if there was no school! / by Andalous Ibrahim ; illustrations by Zahra Amini ; translated by Ghenwa Yehia. First English edition. – Doha, Qatar : Hamad Bin Khalifa University Press, 2022.

pages ; cm

ISBN 978-992-715-599-4

Translation of: ماذا لو اختفت المدرسة!.

1. School -- Juvenile fiction. 2. Children's stories, Arabic, Translations into English. 3. Picture books. I. Amini, Zahra, illustrator. II. Yehia, Ghenwa, translator. III. Title.

PZ10.731. I2713 2022
892.737– dc 23   202228383564

What If There Was No School!

By Andalous Ibrahim

Illustrations by Zahra Amini

Translated by Ghenwa Yehia

Salma and Leila love school.

Salma's favorite subject is science. She loves to impress her friends and teachers with her knowledge. But when it comes down to work, Salma is a bit lazy. She complains about school almost every day!

He older sister, Leila, loves to read. Her mother calls her a bookworm.

One day, Salma came back from school upset. She threw her backpack on the couch, frustrated.

"I have so much homework," she complained. "And after such a long day at school, I am so tired. Why do we even have to go to school every day?!"

Leila looked at her empathetically. She was used to her little sister whining about school.

"We go to sleep early and we get up early just to spend long hours in class," Salma continued to moan.
Leila tried interrupting her, but Salma went on.

"Not to mention that we have to wear this itchy uniform, and follow so many rules all day long!"

Leila wanted to get her sister's mind off of her complaints. "If we want to get rid of something we don't like," Leila began, "we must simply imagine that it doesn't exist."

"So... you want me to imagine a world without school?" Salma asked, suddenly excited.

"Yes," Leila encouraged.

"That would be so cool," Salma agreed delightedly.

"I would sleep in late in the mornings," Salma began. "I'd spend my day playing, drawing, coloring, riding my bike and just having fun!"

"But you would be playing alone because everyone else would be in school," Leila interrupted. "You'd get bored all by yourself!"

"Well," Salma continued, "once you come home, we can play together."

"But I'll be busy with homework and reading," Leila responded.

"I heard that some kids are homeschooled," Salma began. "I wouldn't have to wake up early, or wear a uniform, and I could study at my own pace, and..."

"But Salma, studying from home means studying without the help of teachers or friends. You'll still have assignments, and even tests! It's not as easy as you think," Leila said.

Salma was disappointed.

"Now, it's my turn to imagine school doesn't exist," Leila said.

She closed her eyes and thought for a moment.

"I would definitely be unhappy," she said aloud. "I'd miss my teacher. She teaches us a lot of things, besides math, science and grammar."

"I like my new teacher," Salma replied.

"I would miss seeing my friends every day and listening to their stories," Leila added.

"Yes," Salma agreed. "I would miss Wadha, Mona and Ghalia, my best friends. I'd even miss Ayman, the troublemaker. He makes us laugh so much!"

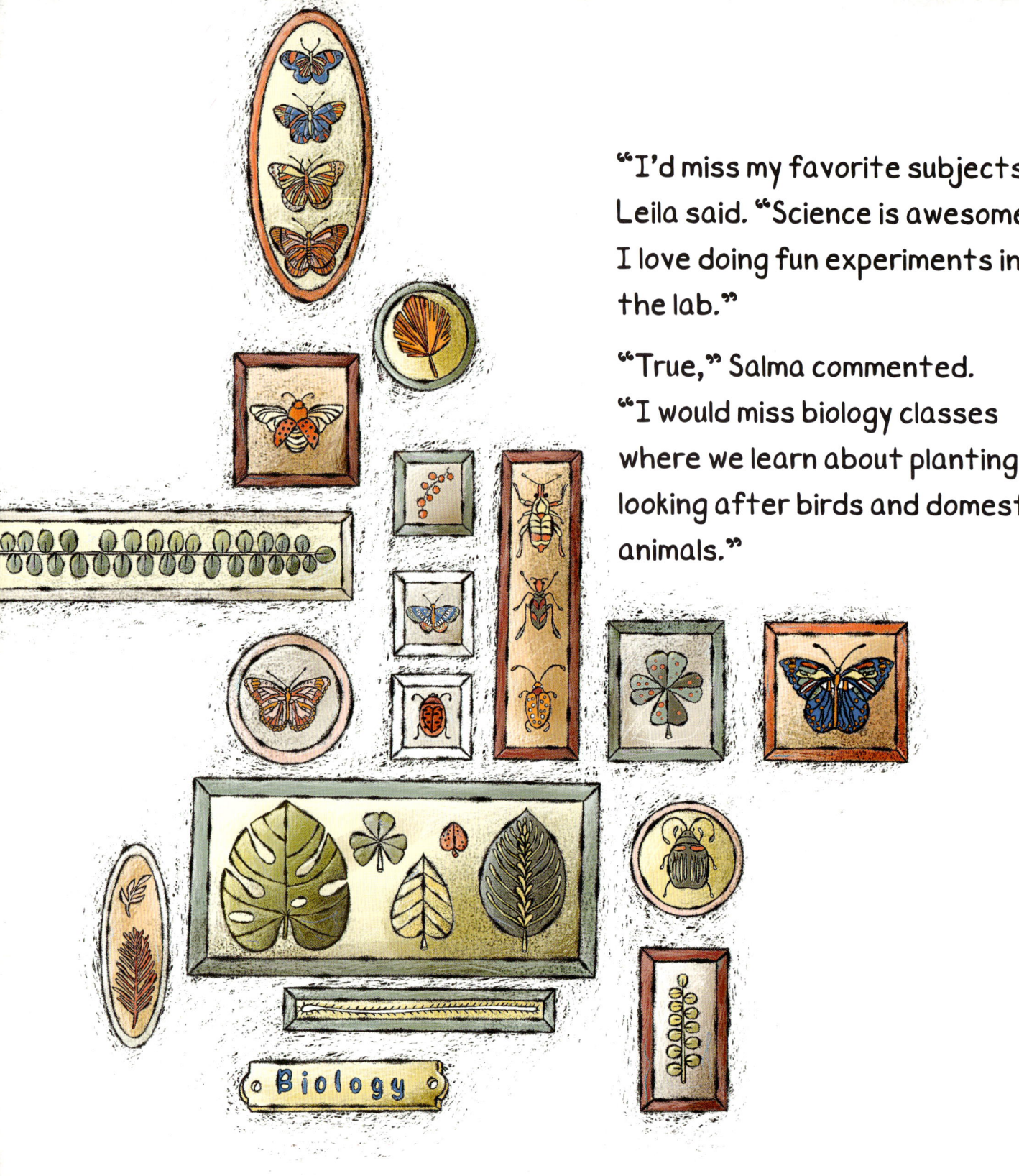

"I'd miss my favorite subjects," Leila said. "Science is awesome! I love doing fun experiments in the lab."

"True," Salma commented. "I would miss biology classes where we learn about planting, looking after birds and domestic animals."

"You and I might have different opinions, Salma," Leila said. "But if we were to spend all our days without school, we would definitely be so bored all the time."

Leila continued as Salma looked at her silently.

"Aren't you going to miss gym class and your swim competitions?" she said.

"Of course! I learned to hold my breath and swim the fastest so I can win," Salma boasted.

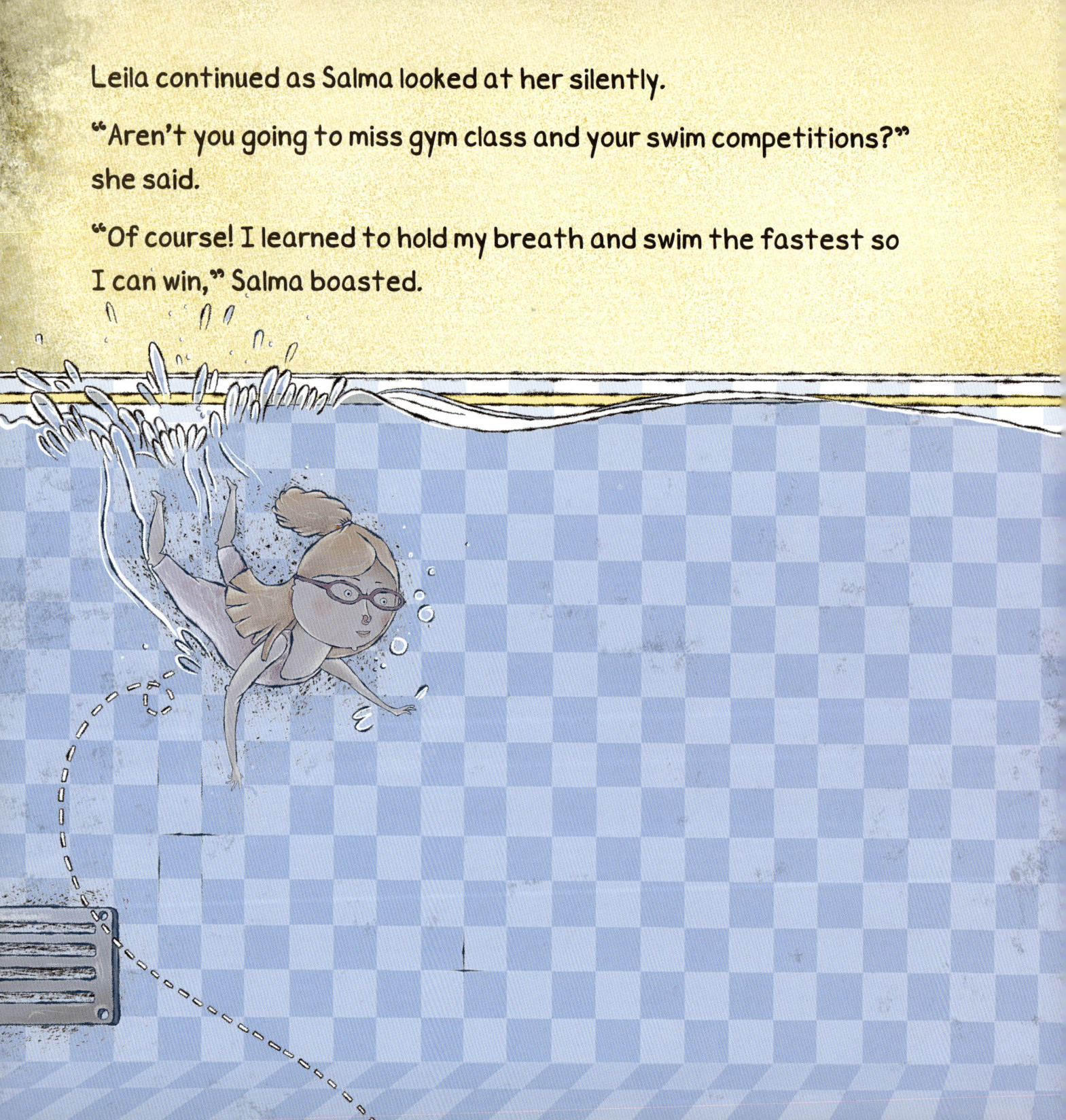

"Amazing!" Leila said.

"But there are too many rules in school. I can't stand it," Salma whined.

"There are rules at home too, Salma," Leila said. "We need rules to keep our school and home safe and comfortable."

Salma wasn't upset anymore, but she wasn't done complaining either. Leila suggested she list everything she would lose by skipping school.

With her eyes closed, Salma counted on her fingers.

"If school is gone, I won't be able to play with my friends.
I won't learn how to grow a garden.
I won't become a good swimmer.
I might even forget my reading, math and science.
I won't be smart anymore and kids might make fun of me for having nothing but empty thoughts in my head."

"I would make the school days shorter with less homework. I would also get rid of that itchy uniform!"

"What a great idea!" Leila said, laughing. "Well, maybe one day you can become a principal and make all of your dreams come true."

The girls agreed to spend some time playing before they got ready for another day of school.

"It seems like there is a lot to lose," Leila said.

Salma nodded in agreement. "Well then, I wish I were the school principal," she added.

"What would you do then?" Leila asked, laughing out loud.